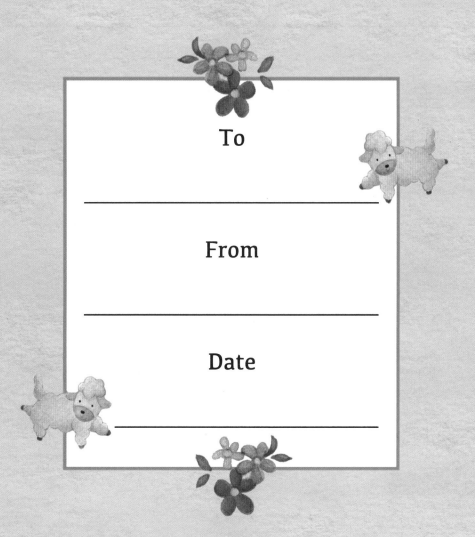

To

_____

From

_____

Date

_____

When Jesus Was a Little Boy

Margi McCombs
Illustrated by Janet Samuel

HARVEST HOUSE PUBLISHERS
EUGENE, OREGON

For Finn and Friends

The child Jesus grew. He became strong and wise, and God blessed him.
Luke 2:40

When Jesus Was a Little Boy

Text copyright © 2013 by Margi McCombs
Artwork copyright © 2013 by Janet Samuel

Published by Harvest House Publishers
Eugene, Oregon 97402
www.harvesthousepublishers.com

ISBN 978-0-7369-5730-4

Original illustrations by Janet Samuel

Design and production by Mary pat Design, Westport, CT

All Scripture quotations are from the Contemporary English Version © 1991, 1992, 1995 by American Bible Society. Used with permission.

Printed in China

13 14 15 16 17 18 19 20 21 /IM/ 10 9 8 7 6 5 4 3 2

When Jesus was a little boy,
He laughed and played like you.

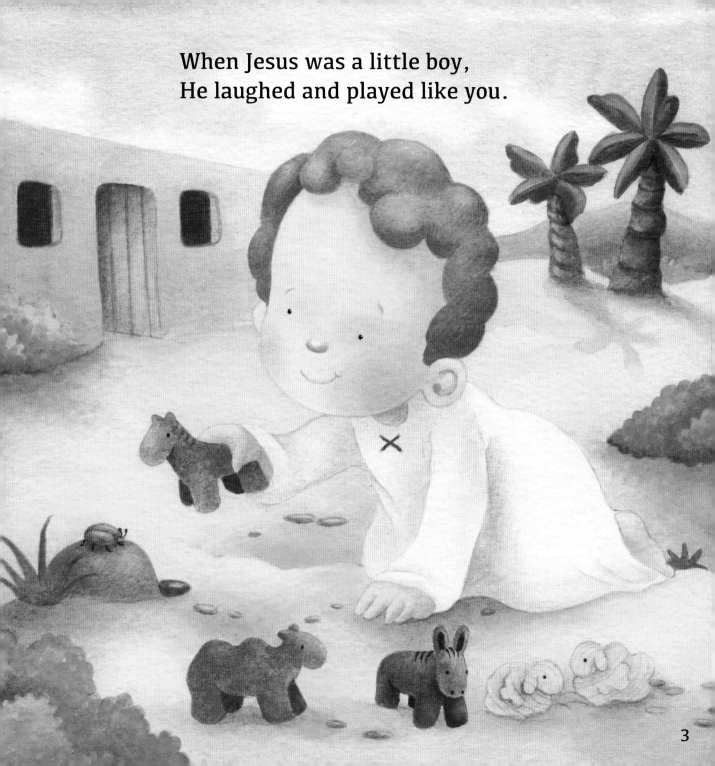

He climbed up trees and skinned his knees.

Sometimes he would cry, too.

When Jesus was a little boy,
He played with lots of friends.

He shared his games and toys with them
And loved to play pretend.

When Jesus was a little boy,
He loved his mommy so.

9

He listened carefully to her words
To learn what he should know.

When Jesus was a little boy,
He asked the question, "Why?"

He was careful to find out first,
Then brave enough to try.

When Jesus was a little boy,
He helped to do the chores.

He did as much as he could do,

And then he did some more!

When Jesus was a little boy,

He loved his animal friends.

He gave them food and lots to drink.
He even cleaned their pens.

When Jesus was a little boy,
He liked to take a rest.
He stopped his work to think and play.
He knew he'd done his best.

When Jesus was a little boy,
He must have liked to sing.

He sang the songs his family loved,
How God made everything.

When Jesus was a little boy,
He would have played with YOU.

He would have been the perfect friend—
So loving, kind, and true.

So Jesus was a little boy,
A child just like you.

31

And you can be like Jesus, too
In everything you do!